Milwaukee Brewers IQ:
The Ultimate Test of True Fandom

JOEL KATTE

Copyright © 2013 Joel Katte
All rights reserved.

No part of this publication may be reproduced, stored in a retrieval system, or transmitted in any form or by any means, electronic, mechanical, recording, or otherwise, without the prior written permission of the author.

ISBN: 9780982675915
Second edition.

Black Mesa Publishing, LLC
Florida

admin@blackmesabooks.com
www.blackmesabooks.com

BLACK MESA IQ TITLES

Mixed Martial Arts (Vol. 1 & 2)
Atlanta Braves
New York Yankees
Georgia Bulldogs
Boston Celtics (Vol. 1 & 2)
Florida Gators
Milwaukee Brewers
St. Louis Cardinals (Vol. 1 & 2)
Major League Baseball
Boston Red Sox (Vol. 1 & 2)
Tampa Bay Rays
Oklahoma Sooners
Texas Longhorns
Texas A&M Aggies
Cincinnati Reds
New England Patriots
West Point
Rock & Roll Music
Buffalo Bills
Kentucky Derby
NHL Hockey
The Beatles
Cleveland Indians
Miami Hurricanes
Baltimore Orioles
Green Bay Packers

CONTENTS

	INTRODUCTION	1
1	SPRING TRAINING	5
2	OPENING DAY	21
3	ALL-STAR GAME	37
4	DOG DAYS OF SUMMER	53
5	OCTOBER BASEBALL	69
6	MINOR LEAGUES	83
7	HALL OF FAME	89
8	THE ULTIMATE STUMPERS	97
	ABOUT THE AUTHOR	101
	GREEN BAY PACKERS IQ PREVIEW	107

> "I led the league in 'Go get 'em next time.'"
> — *Bob Uecker*

INTRODUCTION

Think you know Brewers baseball? Think again. Find out how much you really know about Brewers trivia and find out where you rank among the who's who of diehard Brewers fans. Are you a rookie? Are you a tested, hardcore veteran headed for the Hall of Fame? Or are you a fair-weather fan who will be clearing waivers for your pending release halfway through the book?

We'll let you know.

Test your skills. Wrack your brain. It's the ultimate Milwaukee Brewers IQ test.

Eight chapters, more than 250 questions – that's what you're up against, and we're keeping score.

Think of chapter one as Spring Training, that magical time of year when everything just feels so right with the world … and, when everybody, even the veterans, gets back to the basics. That's what you will find in the first chapter – 45 questions every Brewers fan should know from nine different categories: The Numbers Game, The Rookies, The Legends, The Hitters, The Pitchers, The Managers, Coaches and

Executives, The Fabulous Feats, The Teams and Miscellaneous.

In chapter two the season is underway and you're expected to be in shape and ready to play, so be sure and fine tune your mad-trivia skills in the first chapter, because when the big club breaks camp the last thing you want is to be left behind with the rookies. The categories are the same but the questions are tougher, and the standings count.

In chapter three find out if you make the All-Star team. You have to start the season strong and then maintain a high level of consistency if you want to be on our All-Star team – and chapter three will toss the wannabes like peanut shucks in the wind.

In chapter four it's the Dog Days of Summer. Can you make a push for the postseason or are you going to succumb to the pressure, unable to close the deal? We amp it up even more, and when the dust settles we'll let you know if you're deserving of chapter five.

You have to earn your way to chapter five. This is the postseason. This is where you will find trivia befitting a world champion. This is where legends are made.

And then?

There's still more. One final shot at the ultimate fraternity – that elite class, the ones who make it to the Hall of Fame. In chapter seven, you'll find out if you've earned your plaque for the Brewers IQ Hall of Fame. Don't get too cocky – because if you hit a slump at any point throughout this book, you might find out you've been relegated to the minor leagues in Chapter Six for some rehabilitative work, and if you choke there, you will receive your outright release.

It's your Brewers IQ, the Ultimate Test of True Fandom.

MILWAUKEE BREWERS IQ

Play Ball!

"I've never been much on stats. Usually those things don't cross my mind as much as helping the team win. I've never set goals for myself. The only goal I've ever really thought about is to win the World Series."

— *Robin Yount*

MILWAUKEE BREWERS IQ

1 SPRING TRAINING

This is Spring Training mind you. We're only stretching here. Just trying to get limber after a long winter of chips, couches, remote controls, beverages of choice and the NFL ... I mean there's no sense straining a groin or pulling a hamstring right out of the box. So we'll just start with the basics – numbers every Brewers fan should know something about.

No point in sweating bullets over these questions. If you don't know these then you don't deserve to make the final cut for the Opening Day roster.

Question 1: What Brewer went homer-less in 1,762 at-bats from 1987 until 1991?

Question 2: What pitcher did the Brewers pay $6,750,000 for his 1-3 record in 1993 and his 1-5 record in 1994?

Question 3: Who played 15 seasons for the Brewers, collecting 2,281 hits in 1,856 games?

Question 4: For whom did the Brewers retire the number 19?

Question 5: On August 19, 1995, Wisconsin Governor Tommy Thompson, Milwaukee County Executive Tony Ament, Milwaukee Mayor John Norquist, and Brewers President Bud Selig revealed a financial plan for a new stadium worth what amount?
- a) $200 million
- b) $250 million
- c) $300 million
- d) $350 million

Question 6: What 19-year-old rookie sensation made his Major League debut with the Brewers in 1988? He moved from third base to shortstop to replace an injured Dale Sveum and his first Major League hit was a home run.
- a) Pat Listach
- b) Ernest Riles
- c) Gary Sheffield
- d) Greg Vaughn

Question 7: What Brewer, despite playing in the minor leagues until late May, won the 2007 National League Rookie of the Year award with a .324 batting average and 34 home runs and 97 RBI in only 113 games?
- a) Ryan Braun
- b) Prince Fielder
- c) Corey Hart
- d) Rickie Weeks

Question 8: In 1978, this Brewers rookie hit .273 in 125 games and placed second behind the Tigers Lou Whitaker in Rookie of the Year balloting.

a) Paul Molitor
b) Cecil Cooper
c) Robin Yount
d) Gorman Thomas

Question 9: In 2006, this Brewer led National League rookies with 28 home runs.
a) Ryan Braun
b) Prince Fielder
c) Corey Hart
d) Rickie Weeks

Question 10: Name the rookie phenom who was the third pick overall in the 1973 Major League Baseball draft. (Hall of Famer Dave Winfield was the fourth pick that year.) This Brewer made his Major League debut in April of 1974 and was only 18 years old.
a) Don Money
b) Cecil Cooper
c) George Scott
d) Robin Yount

Question 11: This former Brewer finished his Hall of Fame career with 755 home runs.

Question 12: What Brewers legend had his number 4 retired and went by the nickname "The Ignitor"?

Question 13: What Milwaukee icon was inducted into the Baseball Hall of Fame with a career batting average of .200 and 14 career home runs?

Question 14: Name the famous trio of teammates who compiled a Major League record 6,399 hits during their playing years together.

Question 15: This legend played all of his Major League seasons with the Milwaukee Brewers. When Brewers President Allen H. (Bud) Selig signed him to a three-year contract after this player's 1989 MVP season, he stated, "There is a whole generation of people who grew up watching [him] play for the Brewers. That fact was not lost upon me or a lot of other people. I received a wonderful letter from a teacher in Madison who said the same thing to me. She said that she had grown up watching [him]. She couldn't imagine the Brewers or herself not having that privilege as long as he played. In my mind and my heart, this is what it's all about." Name this legend.

Question 16: On April 28, 2001, this Brewer crushed three home runs to help Ben Sheets record his first Major League victory.
    a) Jeffrey Hammonds
    b) Geoff Jenkins
    c) Jose Hernandez
    d) Richie Sexson

Question 17: What Brewers slugger surpassed Willie Mays as the youngest player ever to hit 50 home runs in a season?

Question 18: What Brewers slugger won a 2009 Louisville Slugger's "Silver Slugger Award." These awards are given to the top hitters at each position in the American and National Leagues according to a vote by Major League coaches and managers.
    a) Ryan Braun

b) Mike Cameron
c) Prince Fielder
d) Casey McGehee

Question 19: Who was the first player to record 3,000 hits for the Milwaukee Brewers?

Question 20: Who holds the Brewers single season RBI record?
a) Ryan Braun
b) Cecil Cooper
c) Prince Fielder
d) Gorman Thomas

Question 21: This Brewers pitcher finished with 324 career wins. However, he only recorded 26 of those wins with Milwaukee. Name this pitching legend.
a) Rollie Fingers
b) Eddie Mathews
c) Warren Spahn
d) Don Sutton

Question 22: Who holds the Brewers record for most strikeouts in one season with 264?
a) Mike Caldwell
b) CC Sabathia
c) Ben Sheets
d) Don Sutton

Question 23: What season did the Brewers pitching staff toss a franchise record 31 consecutive scoreless innings?
a) 1978
b) 1981

c) 1987
d) 1990

Question 24: What Brewer became the first Mexican-born pitcher to win 20 games in a season in the American League?
a) Rickey Bones
b) Teddy Higuera
c) Juan Nieves
d) Jamie Navarro

Question 25: What pitching legend recorded 37 saves for the 2009 Brewers?

Question 26: What manager led the team known as "Bambi's Bombers"?

Question 27: What former Oakland A's manager was hired to manage the Brewers beginning with the 2009 season?
a) Ken Macha
b) Rene Lachemann
c) Davey Lopes
d) Dave Stewart

Question 28: In 2005, the Selig family turned over the Brewers to this Los Angeles financial wizard.
a) Mark Attanasio
b) Warren Buffet
c) Bill Gates
d) Donald Trump

Question 29: After the Brewers exciting 2005 season, considered by some to be their best season since 1992, the organization announced that it would extend a three-year

contract to what executive?
   a) Mark Attanasio
   b) Harry Dalton
   c) Doug Melvin
   d) Wendy Selig-Prieb

Question 30: What Brewers skipper earned his 500th win on August 26, 1998, against the Colorado Rockies? He is the only Brewers manager to accomplish this feat.

Question 31: On June 25, 2005, these two Brewer rookies slugged their first Major League home runs in the same game.
   a) Prince Fielder and Corey Hart
   b) Prince Fielder and Rickie Weeks
   c) Rickie Weeks and JJ Hardy
   d) Rickie Weeks and Corey Hart

Question 32: In 2009, this Brewer led the National League in hits with 203.
   a) Ryan Braun
   b) Prince Fielder
   c) Bill Hall
   d) JJ Hardy

Question 33: Juan Nieves became the first Brewer to throw a no-hitter. He also became the first Puerto Rican-born pitcher to throw a no-hitter in the Major Leagues. What year did Nieves accomplish this feat?
   a) 1986
   b) 1987
   c) 1988
   d) 1989

Question 34: Three times the Milwaukee Brewers have had four representatives in the All-Star Game. The last year they accomplished this feat was 2007. Which player was *not* one of the 2007 All-Stars?
    a) Prince Fielder
    b) Bill Hall
    c) JJ Hardy
    d) Francisco Cordero
    e) Ben Sheets

Question 35: What Brewer holds the franchise record of 18 strikeouts in one game?
    a) Moose Haas
    b) Teddy Higuera
    c) Ben Sheets
    d) Don Sutton

Question 36: Not since 1982 has a team captivated the city of Milwaukee like the 2008 Brewers. Prince Fielder, Ryan Braun, and CC Sabathia led this battling team into its first postseason in 26 years – making for a memorable season. The Brewers finished 90-72. What reigning American League Cy Young Award winner was traded to the Brewers on July 7, 2008, in a deal that General Manager Doug Melvin proved, "We're going for it!"
    a) Roy Halladay
    b) Cliff Lee
    c) CC Sabathia
    d) Johan Santana

Question 37: With only 12 games left in the season, Mark Attanasio's gutsy firing of manager Ned Yost proved to be a winning decision when this interim manager helped the

Brewers win 7 of the last 12 games, clinching the Wild Card for the Brewers first postseason berth since 1982.
   a) Ken Macha
   b) Don Money
   c) Dale Sveum
   d) Cecil Cooper

Question 38: Who hit a walk-off two-run home run during a critical game against the Pittsburgh Pirates on September 23, 2008?
   a) Ryan Braun
   b) Prince Fielder
   c) Bill Hall
   d) JJ Hardy

Question 39: Who hit a walk-off grand slam during another must-win game against the Pittsburgh Pirates on September 25, 2008?
   a) Ryan Braun
   b) Prince Fielder
   c) Bill Hall
   d) JJ Hardy

Question 40: In the do-or-die 2008 regular season finale against the Chicago Cubs, what Brewer belted a go-ahead two-run home run in the eighth to lift the Brewers to a 3-1 win in front of 45,299 fans at Miller Park?
   a) Ryan Braun
   b) Prince Fielder
   c) Bill Hall
   d) JJ Hardy

Question 41: Who in the Brewers organization is known as

"Mr. Baseball"?

Question 42: On June 12, 1997, the Milwaukee Brewers played their first interleague game and became the first American League team to play at this ballpark since the 1945 World Series.
  a) Busch Stadium
  b) Polo Grounds
  c) Shea Stadium
  d) Wrigley Field

Question 43: In 2001, this Brewer hit 45 home runs, tying Gorman Thomas's franchise record. He also came up one short of the Brewers RBI record of 126.
  a) Carlos Lee
  b) John Jaha
  c) Geoff Jenkins
  d) Richie Sexson

Question 44: What year did former home run king Hank Aaron return to Milwaukee as a Brewer? On April 11, Opening Day, Milwaukee declared "Welcome Home, Henry Day" and beat the Cleveland Indians 6-2.
  a) 1973
  b) 1974
  c) 1975
  d) 1976

Question 45: Name the Brewer who joined Hank Greenberg and Stan Musial as the only players to win the MVP award at two different positions.

1 SPRING TRAINING ANSWER KEY

1. Jim Gantner.

2. Teddy Higuera. If you are doing the math that comes out to $3, 375,000 per win.

3. Paul Molitor, 1978-92. His trade to the Blue Jays in 1993 devastated Milwaukee fans. Although fans missed this legend, they were happy to see him win a World Series with the Blue Jays. He finished his 21-year career with his hometown team, the Minnesota Twins. His 3,319 career hits is 9th all-time behind Pete Rose (4,256), Ty Cobb (4,191), Hank Aaron (3,771), Stan Musial (3,630), Tris Speaker (3,514), Carl Yastrzemski (3,419) Cap Anson (3,418) and Honus Wagner (3,415).

4. Robin Yount.

5. B – $250 million. On October 12, 1995, Governor Thompson signed the Stadium Bill into law in County Stadium's centerfield parking lot.

6. C – Gary Sheffield.

7. A – Ryan Braun.

8. A – Paul Molitor.

9. B – Prince Fielder.

10. D – Robin Yount.

11. Hank Aaron.

12. Paul Molitor.

13. Bob Uecker.

14. Jim Gantner, Paul Molitor, and Robin Yount.

15. Robin Yount.

16. B – Geoff Jenkins.

17. Prince Fielder. He hit 50 home runs in 2007 to set the Brewers single season home run record. His father Cecil Fielder hit 51 home runs for the Detroit Tigers in 1990. They are currently the only father/son duo to each hit 50 home runs in a season.

18. A – Ryan Braun.

19. Robin Yount.

20. C – Prince Fielder, with 141. In 2009, Fielder broke Cecil Cooper's record of 126 RBI in a game against the Houston Astros. Interestingly, Cooper, serving as the Houston Astros manager, witnessed Fielder's feat from the visitor's dugout at Miller Park. Cooper and Fielder's paths had previously crossed when Cooper managed in the Brewers minor league system while Fielder was working his way up to the Big Leagues.

21. D – Don Sutton.

22. C – Ben Sheets.

23. D – 1990.

24. B – Teddy Higuera.

25. Trevor Hoffman. He completed 2009 with a Major League record 591 career saves.

26. George Bamberger.

27. A – Ken Macha.

28. A – Mark Attanasio.

29. C – Doug Melvin.

30. Phil Garner.

31. B – Prince Fielder and Rickie Weeks.

32. A – Ryan Braun.

33. B – 1987.

34. B – Bill Hall.

35. C – Ben Sheets.

36. C – CC Sabathia.

37. C – Dale Sveum.

38. B – Prince Fielder.

39. A – Ryan Braun.

40. A – Ryan Braun.

41. Bob Uecker.

42. D – Wrigley Field.

43. D – Richie Sexson.

44. C – 1975.

JOEL KATTE

45. Robin Yount – shortstop in 1982, centerfield in 1989.

MILWAUKEE BREWERS IQ

Got your Spring Training total? Here's how it breaks down:

No drop status in fantasy leagues everywhere
= 40-45

Opening Day starter
= 35-39

You made it to The Show
= 30-34

Utility player at best
= 25-29

Go directly to the Minor Leagues (Ch.6)
= 00-24

Good luck on Opening Day!

"[Paul] Molitor didn't walk across the lake to get here and he didn't change his clothes in the phone booth. He's just a tough hitter."

— *Doc Edwards*

2 OPENING DAY

They all count now, no pressure. You made the roster with the big club and now you're looking forward to earning a seven-figure contract, some major endorsements perhaps, or being a part of the Sunday Conversation on SportsCenter, but most importantly, you're here to help the team earn a chance to play in the playoffs. So game on, let's find out how well you can perform in the clutch after we toss some 95 MPH fastballs your way while mixing in some nasty sliders. The categories stay the same, but the questions are now big league caliber. We're about to find out whether or not you can play this game for a living.

Question 46: What attendance milestone have the Brewers achieved in 2008 and 2009?

Question 47: In 1987, Paul Molitor captivated Major League Baseball with his hitting streak. How many consecutive games did he hit safely in?

Question 48: Who did the Brewers select as the first pick in the 1985 Major League Baseball draft?

Question 49: In 1991, this Brewer hit .325 (fourth best in the American League) with 216 hits and 133 runs scored. Most impressively, he hit .388 with two outs. Although his individual statistics were some of the best of his career, he was quoted as saying, "It's always difficult to talk about a year when things have gone well personally, but when you've been disappointed by what's happened collectively ... The season was a disappointment because as a team we ended up watching baseball in October rather than playing. We were frustrated by another year gone by and another lost opportunity of getting back to the World Series" (Brewers.com). Name this player who was selected as the Brewers 1991 team MVP.

Question 50: Robin Yount holds the Brewers record for most runs scored. How many runs did he score during his 20-year career with Milwaukee?
    a)   1,264
    b)   1,386
    c)   1,593
    d)   1,632

Question 51: In 1985, this Brewers pitcher was named *The Sporting News* Rookie Pitcher of the Year and finished second for the American League Rookie of the Year award. Name this pitcher.
    a)   Teddy Higuera
    b)   Jamie Navarro
    c)   Juan Nieves
    d)   Dan Plesac

Question 52: In 1999, this pitcher was the Brewers first round

draft pick (tenth overall). In 2000, he pitched for the United States National Olympic Team in Sydney, Australia and tossed a complete game shutout in the Gold Medal Game against Cuba. In 2001, he finished 11-10 in his Major League rookie season. Who was this pitcher?
 a) Jeff D'Amico
 b) Doug Davis
 c) Julio Machado
 d) Ben Sheets

Question 53: In 2009, this Brewer hit .301 with 16 home runs and finished fifth in the National League Rookie of the Year Award voting.
 a) Alcides Escobar
 b) Mat Gamel
 c) Jody Gerut
 d) Casey McGehee

Question 54: What Brewers rookie broke Oakland A's slugger Mark McGwire's record for highest slugging percentage (.618) for a rookie?
 a) Ryan Braun
 b) Prince Fielder
 c) Geoff Jenkins
 d) Greg Vaughn

Question 55: Who became the first Brewer to hit a home run in his first Major League game?
 a) Geoff Jenkins
 b) Paul Molitor
 c) Gary Sheffield
 d) Greg Vaughn

Question 56: What Brewer became the first player to have two four-hit games in a single World Series?

Question 57: In addition to his home run prowess, this Brewers legend was known for his tailgating with fans before and after the games. He hit 175 home runs for the Brewers from 1978 to 1982, including 45 homers in 1979. Name this legend.

Question 58: Ned Yost, a former teammate of this Brewers legend, stated in an MLB.com article, "I was drawn by his passion, his love of the game, his energy, the way that he played the game with an all-out style. He was a guy that I could really relate to. I tried to play the game as hard as he did." Who is this Brewers legend that went by the nickname "Gumby"?
    a) Jim Gantner
    b) Charlie Moore
    c) Gorman Thomas
    d) Pete Vuckovich

Question 59: Considered to be one of the founding fathers of relief pitchers, this Brewers legend ended his career with a record 341 saves. (Note: The all-time save record has since been broken multiple times.) Name this pitcher.

Question 60: Who is the first player to be inducted into the Hall of Fame wearing a Brewers hat?

Question 61: What Brewer set a franchise record with 53 doubles in 2004?
    a) Jeff Cirillo
    b) Geoff Jenkins
    c) Lyle Overbay
    d) Richie Sexson

Question 62: Who holds the Brewers record for highest season batting average of .353?
    a) Ryan Braun
    b) Jeff Cirillo

c) Paul Molitor
d) Robin Yount

Question 63: On May 21, 2003, what Brewer hit three home runs in the same game for the second time in his career?
a) Jeromy Burnitz
b) John Jaha
c) Geoff Jenkins
d) Dave Nilsson

Question 64: On May 21, 2005, this Brewer recorded his 1,000th career RBI, helping Doug Davis notch a 6-0 shutout against the Minnesota Twins.
a) Jeff Cirillo
b) Bill Hall
c) Carlos Lee
d) Geoff Jenkins

Question 65: What two Brewer teammates combined for 389 hits in 1989?

Question 66: In 1993, this player became the first pitcher in Brewers history to lead the league in innings pitched with 258.
a) Cal Eldred
b) Graeme Lloyd
c) Jamie Navarro
d) Bill Wegman

Question 67: Who holds the franchise record for most shutouts in one season with six?
a) Mike Caldwell
b) CC Sabathia
c) Ben Sheets
d) Jim Slaton

Question 68: In 1985, this Brewer became the first visiting

pitcher to throw a one-hitter at Yankee Stadium in 17 years.
   a) Moose Haas
   b) Pete Ladd
   c) Pete Vuckovich
   d) Bill Wegman

Question 69: Who pitched the Brewers past the Chicago Cubs in a critical 2008 season finale 3-1 win? After the Brewers win and a Florida Marlins win over the New York Mets, the team clinched its first postseason berth in 26 years.
   a) Dave Bush
   b) Yovanni Gallardo
   c) CC Sabathia
   d) Jeff Suppan

Question 70: What two Brewers each threw a scoreless inning in the 2004 All-Star Game at the Houston Astros' Minute Maid Park?
   a) Ben Sheets and Dan Kolb
   b) Ben Sheets and Chris Capuano
   c) Dan Kolb and Chris Capuano
   d) Ben Sheets and Doug Davis

Question 71: In 1978, this Brewers manager earned *The Sporting News* Manager of the Year award.

Question 72: What Brewers manager helped coach in the 2005 All-Star Game?

Question 73: What Brewers manager owned the tavern Cesar's Inn on 56th Street and National Avenue, a relay throw's distance from County Stadium?
   a) George Bamberger
   b) Harvey Kuenn
   c) Buck Rodgers

d) George Webb

Question 74: Who replaced Harvey Kuenn as manager after the club's 87-75 record in 1983?
   a) George Bamberger
   b) Alex Grammas
   c) Rene Lachemann
   d) Tom Trebelhorn

Question 75: Mark Attanasio's first big move as Brewers owner was to sign this player to a four-year $38.5 million deal in 2005.
   a) Ryan Braun
   b) Prince Fielder
   c) Eric Gagne
   d) Ben Sheets

Question 76: Robin Yount won American League MVP awards in 1982 and 1989. Who is the only other Brewer to win an MVP award?
   a) Cecil Cooper
   b) Prince Fielder
   c) Rollie Fingers
   d) Paul Molitor

Question 77: On May 10, 2001, this Brewer crushed three home runs at Miller Park to help lift the Brew Crew to an 11-1 win over the Chicago Cubs.
   a) Jeromy Burnitz
   b) Jeffrey Hammonds
   c) Geoff Jenkins
   d) Richie Sexson

Question 78: In 2004, this Brewer recorded 70 stolen bases.
   a) Corey Hart
   b) Scott Podsednik

    c) Junior Spivey
    d) Fernando Vina

Question 79: Right before the 1990 All-Star break, the Brewers pounded the California Angels 20-7. Darryl Hamilton hit his first career grand slam. How many runs did the Brewers score in the fifth inning?
    a) 8
    b) 11
    c) 13
    d) 17

Question 80: On July 31, 1990, Nolan Ryan became the 20th pitcher to win 300 games when he defeated the Brewers 11-3 at County Stadium in front of 51,533 fans. Who was the losing pitcher that day for Milwaukee? He gave up five earned runs in 5.1 innings pitched.
    a) Chris Bosio
    b) Teddy Higuera
    c) Jamie Navarro
    d) Bill Wegman

Question 81: There is no more celebrated Brewers squad than the 1982 team that lost to the St Louis Cardinals in Game 7 of the World Series. On June 1, 1982, this manager took over the Brewers on an interim basis. The Brewers were 23-24 and seven games out of first place in the Eastern Division, tied for fifth place. This manager inspired the Brewers to win 72 of their next 115 games to finish the season with a Major League best 95-67 record. Name this celebrated Brewers skipper.

Question 82: In June of 1982, the Brewers won 20 of 27 games. They also set an American League record for most home runs in 15 consecutive games. How many home runs did "Harvey's Wallbangers" crush during this 15-game stretch?

a) 20
b) 25
c) 30
d) 35

Question 83: By how many games did the Brewers win the Eastern Division title?
a) 1
b) 2
c) 3
d) 5

Question 84: On October 3, 1982, what Brewers pitcher picked up the win to clinch the Eastern Division title?
a) Mike Caldwell
b) Jim Slaton
c) Don Sutton
d) Pete Vuckovich

Question 85: True or False: The Brewers were down 0-2 to the California Angels and became only the second team in history to overcome an 0-2 deficit to win the American League Championship Series.

Question 86: In 2006, this Brewers team MVP hit 35 home runs and collected 85 RBI.
a) Prince Fielder
b) Geoff Jenkins
c) Bill Hall
d) Carlos Lee

Question 87: On September 29, 2000, the Milwaukee Brewers played their last game at County Stadium in front of 56,354 fans. The 100-minute closing ceremonies were led by Bob Uecker and included appearances by Hall of Famers Hank

Aaron and Warren Spahn of the Milwaukee Braves, Rollie Fingers and Robin Yount of the Milwaukee Brewers, and Jim Taylor and Willie Davis of the Green Bay Packers. To whom did the Brewers lose their final County Stadium game to 8-1?
- a) Chicago Cubs
- b) St. Louis Cardinals
- c) Cincinnati Reds
- d) Chicago White Sox

Question 88: Who is the Brewer remembered for both his long ball and league-leading strikeouts? In 1987, he became the first player in Major League history to have 100 more strikeouts than RBI (186 strikeouts to 80 RBI).

Question 89: In what year did the Brewers find themselves in an exciting pennant race only to have their postseason dreams come crashing down when the Toronto Blue Jays clinched the American League Eastern Division on the second to last day of the season?
- a) 1989
- b) 1990
- c) 1991
- d) 1992

Question 90: What Brewer holds the franchise record for most stolen bases with 412?
- a) Sixto Lezcano
- b) Paul Molitor
- c) Fernando Vina
- d) Robin Yount

2 OPENING DAY ANSWER KEY

46. They went over the 3,000,000 mark!

47. 39 – only six players in the history of Major League Baseball have had longer streaks. Joe DiMaggio of the New York Yankees (56 games in 1941), Willie Keeler of the Baltimore Orioles (45 and 44 in 1896-97), Pete Rose of the Cincinnati Reds (44 in 1978), Bill Dahlen of the Chicago Colts (42 in 1894), George Sisler of the St. Louis Browns (41 in 1922), and Ty Cobb of the Detroit Tigers (40 in 1911).

48. BJ Surhoff. The Brewers passed on Will Clark (San Francisco Giants), Barry Larkin (Cincinnati Reds), Barry Bonds (Pittsburgh Pirates), Rafael Palmeiro (Chicago Cubs), Randy Johnson (Montreal Expos), David Justice (Atlanta Braves), John Smoltz (Detroit Tigers), and Mark Grace (Chicago Cubs).

49. Paul Molitor.

50. D – 1,632.

51. A – Teddy Higuera.

52. D – Ben Sheets.

53. D – Casey McGehee.

54. A – Ryan Braun (.634).

55. A – Geoff Jenkins – in his Major League debut on April 24, 1998, Jenkins hit a home run against the Giants Orel Hershiser.

56. Robin Yount.

57. Stormin' Gorman Thomas.

58. A – Jim Gantner.

59. Rollie Fingers.

60. Robin Yount.

61. C – Lyle "Ooooooooo" Overbay.

62. C – Paul Molitor, 1987.

63. C – Geoff Jenkins.

64. C – Carlos Lee.

65. Robin Yount and Paul Molitor.

66. A – Cal Eldred.

67. A – Mike Caldwell.

68. A – Moose Haas.

69. C – CC Sabathia.

70. A – Ben Sheets and Dan Kolb.

71. George Bamberger.

72. Ned Yost.

73. B – Harvey Kuenn.

74. C – Rene Lachemann.

75. D – Ben Sheets.

76. C – Rollie Fingers.

77. A – Jeromy Burnitz.

78. B – Scott Podsednik.

79. C – 13.

80. A – Chris Bosio.

81. Harvey Kuenn. Five days after the Brewers lost Game 7 to the Cardinals, Brewers General Manager Harry Dalton dropped the word "interim" from Kuenn's title. In a November 1982 What's Brewing article, Dalton said, "We think it is fitting that Harvey returns to manage the Brewers in 1983. He played a major role in the Milwaukee Brewers' finest season ever, leading them to the American League Championship and a near miss in the seventh game of a World Series. He was just what the doctor ordered." The article went on to report that the reason it took five days before the Brewers announced Kuenn's appointment for the next season was the organization's concern with his health. This courageous manager had overcome heart problems, stomach surgery and a leg amputation.

82. D – 35.

83. A – 1.

84. C – Don Sutton.

85. False – the Brewers became the first team to overcome an 0-2 deficit to win the American League Championship Series.

86. C – Bill Hall.

87. C – Cincinnati Reds.

88. Rob Deer. Deer also had 100 more strikeouts than RBI during his 1991 and 1993 seasons with the Detroit Tigers. With 186 strikeouts in 1987, Deer set a league record that was eventually passed by Jack Cust in 2008. Deer is the easiest person to strikeout in Major League history, averaging a strikeout every 2.56 at-bats. His .220 career batting average is one of the lowest of all-time. On a positive note, Deer's patience and large presence at the plate resulted in many walks allowing him to have a respectable .324 career on-base percentage. He ended his career with 230 home runs.

89. D – 1992.

90. B – Paul Molitor.

Got your Opening Day total? Here's how it breaks down:

MLB Player of the Month for April
= 40-45

Scott Boras wants to represent you
= 35-39

You're still in The Show
= 30-34

Struggling to get playing time
= 25-29

You just got sent down to the Minor Leagues (Ch.6) for some rehabilitation
= 00-24

Good luck in the All-Star balloting!

"When you gave him [Don Sutton] the ball you knew one thing – your pitcher was going to give you everything he had."
— *Tommy Lasorda*

3 ALL-STAR GAME

So you want to be an All-Star, no problem. All you have to do is bring your "A" game to the park every day, your absolute best, day in, day out, because only a select few make it to that upper echelon where you hear things like "franchise player" or "future Hall of Famer." Oh, and one more thing . . . you have to be better than almost everyone else to make it, which means for some of you, well, your "A" game might not be enough. You better work hard. I mean, really hard. You do well here and you will not only have shown us something special, but you will also have earned yourself some well-deserved recognition. Let's play ball!

Question 91: How old was Robin Yount when he made his Major League Baseball debut with the Milwaukee Brewers?

Question 92: What Brewers catcher made his debut in 1980 after an impressive .309 batting average and an astounding .997 fielding percentage for the Brewers Class-AAA Vancouver

Canadians? In 1981 he was quoted by the Brewers magazine *What's Brewing* as saying, "I'm a lot happier to go out there, call a good game, throw one or two runners out and block some balls in the dirt than if I were to go out and go 4-for-4 and not play well behind the plate. I'd rather play well behind the plate and take an 0 for 4. You look around the league at all the good catchers, who've been around ten, twelve, fifteen years, and they are all excellent defensively." In the same article, he stated, "I don't have any goals for this season. The only goal I set is to do the best job I can possibly do and to help Milwaukee get into the World Series any way I can. Anything I can do, anything that helps us get to the World Series is my goal. I know we have the team that can do it."

Question 93: In what year did Bernie Brewer, Bonnie Brewer, and organist Frank Charles help the Brewers draw over one million fans for the first time?
    a)   1970
    b)   1971
    c)   1972
    d)   1973

Question 94: Who was hit by 95 pitches during his Brewers career?
    a)   Cecil Cooper
    b)   Paul Molitor
    c)   Jim Gantner
    d)   Geoff Jenkins

Question 95: Who holds the Brewers season record for most strikeouts averaged per nine innings pitched with 10.03?
    a)   Rollie Fingers
    b)   CC Sabathia

c) Ben Sheets
d) Bill Wegman

Question 96: Name the Brewer who was selected in the first round of the 1982 draft and made his Major League debut with the Brewers in 1986. Hint: He eventually became a Brewers manager.

Question 97: This Brewers rookie was named to the 1985 Topps All-Rookie team and finished third in the Rookie of the Year voting.
a) Teddy Higuera
b) Joey Meyer
c) Ernest Riles
d) B.J. Surhoff

Question 98: Who did the Seattle Pilots select as their first round pick in the 1969 Major League Baseball draft?
a) Don Money
b) Charlie Moore
c) Gorman Thomas
d) Darrell Porter

Question 99: This Brewers first round draft pick won his Major League debut in 1991, becoming the first Brewers pitcher to win his Major League debut since Rickey Keaton in 1980.
a) Kevin Brown
b) Cal Eldred
c) Darren Holmes
d) Julio Machado

Question 100: This former University of Miami Hurricane was

a Brewers first round draft pick (fifth overall).

Question 101: What aging slugger hit .289 with 21 home runs and 92 RBI for the Brewers in 1990?

Question 102: For whom did the Brewers retire the number 44?

Question 103: What two Brewers played in the 1975 All-Star Game held at Milwaukee County Stadium?
- a) Hank Aaron and George Scott
- b) Hank Aaron and Don Money
- c) Hank Aaron and Jim Slaton
- d) George Scott and Don Money

Question 104: What Brewers legend used to park his Corvette inside County Stadium?

Question 105: What Brewer legend drove in the game-winning run Game 5 of the 1982 American League Championship Series to lift the Brewers over the California Angels and send them to the World Series for the only time in franchise history?
- a) Cecil Cooper
- b) Paul Molitor
- c) Gorman Thomas
- d) Robin Yount

Question 106: What 6' 8" slugger hit 133 home runs and knocked in 398 RBI for the Brewers from 2000 until 2003?

Question 107: What Brewers catcher hit for the cycle on October 1, 1980, helping the Brewers beat the California Angels 10-7. (Paul Molitor and Ben Oglivie also added four hits each in the game.)

a) Andy Etchebarren
b) Charlie Moore
c) Ted Simmons
d) Ned Yost

Question 108: Who ranks third behind Robin Yount and Paul Molitor on the Brewers all-time list with 1,815 hits?
a) Cecil Cooper
b) Jim Gantner
c) Geoff Jenkins
d) Don Money

Question 109: What Brewer hit a franchise record 16 triples in 1979?
a) Sal Bando
b) Sixto Lezcano
c) Paul Molitor
d) Robin Yount

Question 110: Which hitter demonstrated incredible patience at the plate when he walked a franchise record 99 times in one season? His record stood until 2009 when it was broken by Prince Fielder, who walked 110 times.
a) Jeromy Burnitz
b) Cecil Cooper
c) Dave Parker
d) Gorman Thomas

Question 111: Who holds the Brewers record for most wins in one season with 22?
a) Mike Caldwell
b) CC Sabathia
c) Ben Sheets

d) Jim Slaton

Question 112: What reliever was the Brewers lone representative in the 2000 All-Star Game?
   a) Jeff D'Amico
   b) Steve Woodard
   c) Jamey Wright
   d) Bob Wickman

Question 113: Who holds the Brewers record for most career wins with 117?
   a) Mike Caldwell
   b) Ben Sheets
   c) Jim Slaton
   d) Moose Haas

Question 114: Who holds the Brewers record for most career losses with 121?
   a) Mike Caldwell
   b) Ben Sheets
   c) Jim Slaton
   d) Moose Haas

Question 115: What ace holds the Brewers single season saves record with 44?
   a) Francisco Cordero
   b) Rollie Fingers
   c) Trevor Hoffman
   d) Dan Plesac

Question 116: Which Brewers General Manager helped lead the Brewers to nine winning seasons from 1978 to 1991?
   a) Harry Dalton

b) Doug Melvin
c) Bud Selig
d) Ted Thompson

Question 117: This coach was originally hired as a spring training and minor league batting instructor in 1971, but quickly moved up to work as the Brewers hitting coach.

Question 118: In 1978, George Bamberger was *The Sporting News* Manager of the Year. What was the team's record that season?
   a) 91-71
   b) 93-69
   c) 88-74
   d) 86-76

Question 119: What former member of the 1982 World Series team has also coached in the Brewers minor league system with the Beloit Snappers (A), Huntsville Stars (AA), and Nashville Sounds (AAA)?
   a) Cecil Cooper
   b) Don Money
   c) Ted Simmons
   d) Ned Yost

Question 120: What Brewer hit .290 with 34 home runs and 115 RBI in his 1978 All-Star season and later went on to a successful hitting coach career, helping the Toronto Blue Jays win back-to-back World Series titles in 1992 and 1993. Under his tutelage in 1993, Blue Jays hitters John Olerud, Paul Molitor, and Roberto Alomar finished first, second, and third respectively for highest American League batting averages.
   a) Sal Bando

b) Larry Hisle
c) Don Money
d) Ned Yost

Question 121: Prince Fielder became the fifth player in franchise history to play 162 games in a season when he accomplished the feat in 2009. Which of the following is *not* one of the other four players who have accomplished this feat?
  a) Carlos Lee
  b) Paul Molitor
  c) Richie Sexson
  d) Gorman Thomas
  e) Robin Yount

Question 122: What Brewer became only the 12th player in American League history to hit two home runs in the same inning on May 17, 1996, against the Minnesota Twins at the Hubert H. Humphrey Metrodome?

Question 123: What slugger became the first Brewer since Cecil Cooper in 1983 to have a batting average of .300 with 30 home runs and 100 RBI in a season?
  a) Jeromy Burnitz
  b) John Jaha
  c) Geoff Jenkins
  d) Dave Nilsson

Question 124: Which Brewer won eight Gold Glove awards throughout his career? Note: Not all awards were won while playing for the Brewers.
  a) Cecil Cooper
  b) Jim Gantner
  c) Don Money

d) George Scott

Question 125: On September 9, 1992, Robin Yount collected his 3,000th hit, becoming only the 17th player in Major League history to accomplish this feat. He accomplished this in his last at-bat of the home series against what opposing Cleveland Indians pitcher?
a) Jose Mesa
b) Charles Nagy
c) Eric Plunk
d) Ted Power

Question 126: The 1987 Brewers – also known as "Team Streak" – provided Milwaukee with an exciting spring, an unforgettable Easter, and a memorable season. How many games in a row did the Brewers win to start the 1987 season?
a) 15
b) 14
c) 13
d) 12

Question 127: On April 15, 1987, this pitcher threw a no-hitter for the Brewers' ninth consecutive win to start the season. He finished the season with a 14-8 record.
a) Teddy Higuera
b) Jamie Navarro
c) Juan Nieves
d) Mike Caldwell

Question 128: Perhaps the most legendary home run in Brewers history is the Easter Sunday walk-off home run hit on April 19, 1987, that lifted the Brewers past the Texas Rangers 6-4 for their 12th consecutive win to start the season. Who hit

this legendary blast?
- a) Jim Gantner
- b) Bill Spiers
- c) Paul Molitor
- d) Dale Sveum

Question 129: What was the Brewers record before they lost their second game of the season?
- a) 13-1
- b) 15-1
- c) 17-1
- d) 19-1

Question 130: The 1987 Brewers finished the season with an impressive 91-71 record. They finished in what place in the American League East?
- a) First
- b) Second
- c) Third
- d) Fourth

Question 131: What franchise was purchased to create the Milwaukee Brewers?

Question 132: In 2006, what three Brewers were named to the All-Star team?

Question 133: On February 21, 2001, Milwaukee County Stadium was demolished. What is the name of the Little League field that is on the site of County Stadium's old infield?
- a) Dalton's Diamond
- b) Hank's Field
- c) Helfaer Field

d) Harvey's Field

Question 134: What was the nickname given to the 1982 World Series against the St. Louis Cardinals?

Question 135: In 2009, the Brewers owned first place from mid-May through July 4, after their clubbing of the Chicago Cubs at Wrigley Field. What was their final season record?
a) 84-78
b) 80-82
c) 82-80
d) 78-84

3 ALL-STAR GAME ANSWER KEY

91. 18 – *LA Times* sportswriter Jeff Prugh, in the November 1974 edition of *Baseball Digest*, reported, "Robin Yount has an adventure-serial name and choir-boy looks and may well be the finest motorcycle-racing, golf-playing baseball player ever to emerge from the playgrounds of Woodland Hills, California. He comes across as the classic hero of Ralph Henry Barbour fiction: the lean, humble, gracefully athletic Superkid who leaped from prep school to the Major Leagues in a single bound."

92. Ned Yost.

93. D – 1973.

94. D – Geoff Jenkins.

95. C – Ben Sheets.

96. Dale Sveum.

97. C – Ernest Riles.

98. C – Gorman Thomas.

99. B – Cal Eldred.

100. Ryan Braun.

101. Dave "The Cobra" Parker. After one season with Milwaukee, Parker was traded to the California Angels for young prospect Dante Bichette.

102. Hank Aaron.

103. A – Hank Aaron and George Scott.

104. Robin Yount.

105. A – Cecil Cooper.

106. Richie Sexson, who represented Milwaukee in the 2002 and 2003 All-Star Games.

107. B – Charlie Moore.

108. A – Cecil Cooper.

109. C – Paul Molitor.

110. A – Jeromy Burnitz.

111. A – Mike Caldwell.

112. D – Bob Wickman, who was born in Green Bay, WI and played baseball for UW-Whitewater. He finished the 2000 season with 30 saves and a 3.10 ERA.

113. C – Jim Slaton.

114. C – Jim Slaton.

115. A – Francisco Cordero.

116. A – Harry Dalton.

117. Harvey Kuenn.

118. B – 93-69, the Brewers finished the season 54-27 (.667) at

County Stadium and were 21-9 in June.

119. B – Don Money.

120. B – Larry Hisle, who currently works for the Brewers organization as the manager of their Youth Outreach program. He is also the president of the youth mentoring program Major League Mentoring in Milwaukee.

121. B – Paul Molitor.

122. Dave Nilsson.

123. B – John Jaha, 1996.

124. D – George Scott; Boston Red Sox, 1967-68, 1974; Milwaukee Brewers 1972-76.

125. A – Jose Mesa.

126. C – 13.

127. C – Juan Nieves.

128. D – Dale Sveum.

129. C – 17-1.

130. C – Third.

131. Seattle Pilots.

132. Carlos Lee, Derrick Turnbow, and Chris Capuano.

133. C – Helfaer Field.

134. "Suds Series".

135. B – 80-82.

Got your All-Star total? Here's how it breaks down:

Most fan votes & All-Star Game MVP
= 40-45

Made the team and won the Home Run Derby
= 35-39

You made it in the final fan vote
= 30-34

You're the guy that got overlooked this year
= 25-29

All-Star? Uh, no ... back to the Minors (Ch. 6)
= 00-24

Good luck down the stretch!

"He's [Cecil Cooper] one of the finest gentlemen I've ever known. I loved having him as a player."
— *Bud Selig*

4 DOG DAYS OF SUMMER

The season really heats up now. The Mid-Summer Classic is behind us, the trade deadline is rapidly approaching, and the race for the postseason is in full throttle. It's the Dog Days of Summer. This is when gritty veterans knock in game-winning runs for walk-off win celebrations while the weak endure painful late summer slumps and begin to fade from contention. Test yourself here and find out if you are a "Gamer," that rare breed of player who just plain knows how to win – or who refuses to lose – who achieves baseball immortality with his clutch exploits on the field, at the time of year when every action is magnified, and when his team and its fans need a hero to lift their city. Think you're that kind of player? We're about to find out ... it's the Dog Days.

Question 136: On July 17, 1991, the Brewers beat the Seattle Mariners 6-1 at County Stadium. Bill Wegman pitched a complete game gem allowing no earned runs. The Brewers batters also set a single game record for most walks in one

game. How many times did Mariners pitchers Randy Johnson, Russ Swan, and Mike Jackson walk Brewers batters?
   a) 12
   b) 15
   c) 17
   d) 20

Question 137: How many Hall of Famers played for the Milwaukee Brewers?
   a) 4
   b) 5
   c) 6
   d) 7

Question 138: How many days did the 2007 Brewers lead or share first place in the National League Central?
   a) 40
   b) 70
   c) 100
   d) 130

Question 139: On April 20, 1993, Robin Yount collected his 200th career hit against the Minnesota Twins. What was significant about this feat?
   a) Yount grew up in Minnesota
   b) Yount's hit happened to be a game-winning grand slam
   c) Yount became the first person in history to collect at least 200 career hits against every team he played against
   d) Yount's hit was ruled a double after it hit the ceiling of the Hubert H. Humphrey Metrodome

MILWAUKEE BREWERS IQ

Question 140: In 1978 and 1979, the Brewers went 213 consecutive games without . . . what?
a) Running out of Secret Stadium Sauce
b) Being shut out
c) Striking out ten or more times in a game
d) Committing three errors in a game

Question 141: Who was the first sausage race winner at Miller Park?

Question 142: What Brewers pitching prospect made his Major League debut June 20, 1989? Hint: He went on to record 17 wins for the Brewers in 1992.

Question 143: In 1976, this Brewer pitcher was named to the Topps All-Rookie Team.

Question 144: Name the Brewers 1987 first round draft pick who made his Major League debut in 1989.

Question 145: In 1985, this Brewer finished second in the American League Rookie of the Year voting while *The Sporting News* named him Rookie Pitcher of the Year.

Question 146: Hank Aaron played for the Milwaukee Braves from 1954 until 1965. In 1957, he hit .322 with 44 home runs and 132 RBI, helping the Braves win the World Series. He returned to Milwaukee to play for the Brewers in his final two seasons. What two years did he play for the Brewers?

Question 147: For whom did the Brewers retire the number 34?

Question 148: Who was not one of the first three non-Brewers

to be inducted into Miller Park's "Walk of Fame" located on the plaza near the statues of Hank Aaron and Robin Yount? Each honoree is represented by a granite-shaped home plate placed in the ground.
- a) Johnny Logan
- b) Eddie Mathews
- c) Boston and Milwaukee Braves executive John Quinn
- d) Warren Spahn

Question 149: This Brewers legend was named to three consecutive All-Star Games in 1976, 1977, and 1978.

Question 150: This Brewers legend was a part of 1,180 double plays, the most in Brewers history.
- a) Cecil Cooper
- b) Jim Gantner
- c) George C. Scott
- d) Paul Molitor

Question 151: Who holds the franchise record for highest career batting average at .307?
- a) Jeff Cirillo
- b) Cecil Cooper
- c) Paul Molitor
- d) Robin Yount

Question 152: What Brewer was hit by 25 pitches in one season?
- a) Jeromy Burnitz
- b) Cecil Cooper
- c) Dave Parker
- d) Fernando Vina

Question 153: What Brewers slugger hit a record 14 sacrifice flies in one season?
a) Jeromy Burnitz
b) Cecil Cooper
c) Dave Parker
d) Gorman Thomas

Question 154: What player hit over .300 seven times during his 11 years with the Brewers?
a) Cecil Cooper
b) Paul Molitor
c) Don Money
d) George Scott

Question 155: This Brewers slugger became the first person in Major League history to hit more than 30 home runs and steal more than 30 bases in one season.
a) Paul Molitor
b) Tommy Harper
c) Joey Meyer
d) Robin Yount

Question 156: What pitcher represented Milwaukee in the 1994 All-Star Game? He finished the season with a 10-9 record and 3.43 ERA.
a) Ricky Bones
b) Cal Eldred
c) Graeme Lloyd
d) Bill Wegman

Question 157: What pitcher led the '78 Brewers with 22 wins, a 2.36 ERA, and 131 strikeouts?

Question 158: That same pitcher set the Brewers record for most complete games in 1978. How many complete games did he pitch?
 a) 15
 b) 18
 c) 21
 d) 23

Question 159: What pitcher holds the Brewers record for lowest bases on balls average per nine innings pitched?
 a) Chuck Crim
 b) Dan Plesac
 c) Ben Sheets
 d) Don Sutton

Question 160: Who holds the single season record for most games pitched with 83?
 a) Todd Coffey
 b) Chuck Crim
 c) Doug Henry
 d) Ken Sanders

Question 161: Before this Brewer became a manager, he collected 2,092 hits during his 15 Major League seasons. He also posted an impressive .303 lifetime batting average.
 a) Phil Garner
 b) Harvey Kuenn
 c) Davey Lopes
 d) Ned Yost

Question 162: What Brewers hitting coach helped Gary Sheffield hit .294 in 1990? Hint: He is also known for getting hit by 267 pitches during his playing career.

Question 163: Who did Harvey Kuenn replace as manager in June of 1982? Hint: He was criticized at times for over-managing and doing too many trick plays.
a) George Bamberger
b) Alex Grammas
c) Rene Lachemann
d) Buck Rodgers

Question 164: Before George Bamberger was appointed manager of the Brewers in 1978, he was the pitching coach for what team?

Question 165: Whose managerial debut resulted in a 3-3 season opening tie against the Cincinnati Reds?
a) Phil Garner
b) Davey Lopes
c) Ken Macha
d) Ned Yost

Question 166: This four-time All-Star held the Major League record for consecutive errorless games (88) and consecutive errorless chances (261).
a) Jim Gantner
b) Don Money
c) Sixto Lezcano
d) Robin Yount

Question 167: What amazing feat did pitcher Jim Colborn accomplish at Memorial Stadium during the Brewers 1-0 loss to the Baltimore Orioles on September 27, 1974?
a) He struck out the side three times
b) He struck out four batters in one inning
c) He turned an unassisted triple play

d) He pitched 13 scoreless innings

Question 168: On May 15, 2001, the Milwaukee Brewers set a franchise record for most extra-base hits in their 14-10 ten-inning win over the Philadelphia Phillies. Of their 22 hits on the day, how many were for extra bases?
   a) 9
   b) 10
   c) 12
   d) 13

Question 169: Who is the only Brewer to be involved in two triple plays?
   a) Jeff Cirillo
   b) Jim Gantner
   c) Pat Listach
   d) Ernest Riles

Question 170: What Brewers rookie became only the fourth Major League player since 1900 to hit .300, steal 40 bases and score 100 runs? Remarkably, he hit a home run in his last at-bat of the season to score his 100th run and join Jimmy Barrett (Cincinnati Reds, 1900), Shoeless Joe Jackson (Chicago White Sox, 1911), and Ichiro Suzuki (Seattle Mariners, 2001) in the record books.
   a) Paul Molitor
   b) Pat Listach
   c) Scott Podsednik
   d) Fernando Vina

Question 171: The Brewers ended the 1981 strike-shortened season with a 62-47 record, which was good enough for a postseason matchup against the New York Yankees in the

American League Division Series (ALDS). It was the first time that division leaders from two halves of the season played for the opportunity to appear in the American League Championship Series. The Brewers lost the first two games of the ALDS to the Yankees at County Stadium, but then battled back to win the next two games played at Yankee Stadium. The Brewers lost the series in Game 5, 7-3. Who was the losing pitcher in Game 5 for the Brewers?
- a) Mike Caldwell
- b) Rollie Fingers
- c) Moose Haas
- d) Pete Vuckovich

Question 172: What pitcher finished the 1981 season with a 14-4 record and a 3.55 ERA?
- a) Mike Caldwell
- b) Moose Haas
- c) Jim Slaton
- d) Pete Vuckovich

Question 173: Name the Brewers pitcher who earned the 1981 Cy Young Award.

Question 174: Who managed the 1981 Brewers?

Question 175: Despite playing in only 103 games, this Brewers slugger finished the 1981 season with 21 home runs.
- a) Cecil Cooper
- b) Ben Oglivie
- c) George Scott
- d) Gorman Thomas

Question 176: What Brewers pitcher once allowed 14 earned

runs in one game?
a) Chris Bosio
b) Mark Clear
c) Mark Knudson
d) Bill Travers

Question 177: What year did the Brewers set franchise records at the time with 203 home runs, 774 runs, 2,535 total bases, and a .448 slugging percentage?
a) 1978
b) 1980
c) 1982
d) 2007

Question 178: In 1977, what Brewer infielder playing for the Class-AAA Spokane Indians filled in for an ill Gorman Thomas in centerfield? This player went on to commit five errors. He had two dropped fly balls, botched two ground balls, and a throwing debacle.
a) Sal Bando
b) Jim Gantner
c) Paul Molitor
d) Lenn Sakata

Question 179: After this beloved Brewer passed away in 1988, the team wore a patch with his initials on their uniform to honor his legacy. He was a West Allis, Wisconsin, native and played baseball for University of Wisconsin-Madison. Who was this beloved Brewer and UW Badger?

Question 180: On June 8, 2004, the Brewers snuck out a 1-0 17-inning win over the Anaheim Angels at Edison International Stadium. How many Brewers did Anaheim

Angels hurlers Kelvim Escobar, Francisco Rodriquez, Scot Shields, Kevin Gregg, and Ramon Ortiz combine to strike out?
- a) 20
- b) 23
- c) 26
- d) 27

4 DOG DAYS OF SUMMER ANSWER KEY

136. B – 15. Randy Johnson walked ten batters in four innings.

137. B – 5. Hank Aaron, Rollie Fingers, Paul Molitor, Don Sutton, and Robin Yount (Bob Uecker is in the Hall of Fame but he never played for the Brewers.)

138. D – 130.

139. C – Yount became the first person in history to collect at least 200 career hits against every team he played.

140. B – Being shut out.

141. Bratwurst! "They [the city of Milwaukee] have the best bratwurst and the best tailgate parties in all of baseball here [Milwaukee County Stadium]." – Author Philip J. Lowry in *Green Cathedrals* (1992)

142. Jamie Navarro.

143. Jerry Augustine.

144. Bill Spiers.

145. Teddy Higuera.

146. 1975 and 1976.

147. Rollie Fingers.

148. A – Johnny Logan.

149. Don Money. Dan Plesac was the only other Brewer to accomplish this feat (1987-89).

150. A – Cecil Cooper.

151. A – Jeff Cirillo.

152. D – Fernando Vina.

153. C – Dave Parker.

154. A – Cecil Cooper.

155. B – Tommy Harper.

156. A – Ricky Bones.

157. Mike Caldwell.

158. Mike Caldwell threw 23 complete games in 1978.

159. C – Ben Sheets, 1.22 in 2004.

160. D – Ken Sanders.

161. B – Harvey Kuenn.

162. Don Baylor.

163. D – Buck Rodgers.

164. Baltimore Orioles.

165. B – Davey Lopes.

166. B – Don Money.

167. D – He pitched 13 scoreless innings.

168. C – 12.

169. A – Jeff Cirillo.

170. C – Scott Podsednik.

171. C – Moose Haas.

172. D – Pete Vuckovich.

173. Rollie Fingers, who opened the season in front of Cleveland with a save and finished the shortened season with a 6-3 record, 1.04 ERA, and 28 saves. Fingers became the first relief pitcher in history to win the American League MVP Award. He also won his fourth Rolaids Relief Man of the Year Award and *The Sporting News* Fireman of the Year Award. Fingers also collected the Joe Cronin Award for his distinguished service.

174. Buck Rodgers.

175. D – Gorman Thomas.

176. D – Bill Travers. He also allowed a club record 18 hits in the game!

177. B – 1980.

178. B – Jim Gantner.

179. "H.K." Harvey Kuenn.

180. C – 26. Geoff Jenkins went 0 for 7 with six strikeouts.

Got your Dog Days total? Here's how it breaks down:

Won the Pennant and NLCS MVP honors
= 40-45

Won the Pennant in a thrilling Game 7
= 35-39

Division Champion
= 30-34

Late season slump but you got the Wild Card
= 25-29

Sitting home this October
= 00-24

Good luck in the World Series!

"He's [Rollie Fingers] the type of pitcher who has command of all his pitches … he knows he's going to get them out. He gives me a lot of confidence when he's out there."

— *Rene Lachemann*

5 OCTOBER BASEBALL

It all comes down to this. You spent your childhood dreaming of this moment.

It's October baseball.

This is your one chance at baseball immortality. You're the underdog. No one expected you to make it this far, but at least to this point you've proved everyone wrong. The only thing left to prove is that you have what it takes to be a world champion. No need to be nervous – although, millions are watching and a blunder now might result in you being pegged as the next Bill Buckner. Focus in and hit 'em where they ain't!

Question 181: What Brewers pitcher allowed a franchise record 36 home runs in one season?
  a) Chris Capuano
  b) Wayne Franklin
  c) Clyde Wright
  d) Derrick Turnbow

Question 182: In 1991, Paul Molitor led off with a home run

six times, tying the franchise record. Name the other Brewer who had six lead off home runs in 1970.
a) Danny Walton
b) Tommy Harper
c) Mike Hegan
d) Ted Savage

Question 183: Thoughts of free George Webb hamburgers entered the minds of fans when the Brewers won ten straight games for the first time since 1988 during this season.
a) 2002
b) 2003
c) 2005
d) 2008

Question 184: Who has pitched 2,025.1 innings for the Brewers, the most in franchise history?

Question 185: What pitcher, despite his pathetic 8-18 record, pitched a one-hitter, two-hitter, and three-hitter in the same season?

Question 186: What did Bernie Brewer (Milt Mason age 69) vow his rookie season in 1970?

Question 187: In 1971, *The Sporting News* named this Brewer Rookie Pitcher of the Year.

Question 188: What Brewer became the first Australian pitcher in Major League history? Hint: Brewers Australian catcher Dave Nilsson caught him in 1994.

Question 189: What rookie made his Major League debut by tossing eight innings of one-hit baseball while striking out 12 batters to out duel Roger Clemens on July 28, 1997?

Question 190: This Brewer was selected in the first round of the 1983 draft from North Carolina State University.

Question 191: What two players wore a Brewer uniform in five All-Star Games?

Question 192: Who won five Gold Glove Awards as a Brewer?

Question 193: What Brewer recorded his 3,000th career strikeout against the Cleveland Indians on June 24, 1983, becoming only the eighth pitcher to achieve that milestone? He also became the first pitcher to record 100 strikeouts in 19 consecutive seasons.

Question 194: What Brewers pitcher was named *The Sporting News* Fireman of the Year after winning seven games and recording 31 saves in 1971?

Question 195: What Brewers legend threw a franchise record 19 career shutouts?

Question 196: Rank the following home run hitters in order of most career home runs as a Brewer: Cecil Cooper, Geoff Jenkins, Ben Oglivie, Gorman Thomas, and Robin Yount.

Question 197: Who became the first Milwaukee Brewer to hit for the cycle on September 3, 1976?

Question 198: Who is believed to be the first Brewers fan favorite? In 1970, the franchise's first season, he hit .321 with seven home runs and 20 RBI in the month of April.

Question 199: What single game record did Brewers hitters Jim Wohlford, Sal Bando, Robin Yount, Tony Muser, and Dick

Davis set in the Brewers 10-5 win over the Toronto Blue Jays at Exhibition Stadium on July 30, 1978?

Question 200: What Brewer became the first Major Leaguer in history to hit two Opening Day grand slams?

Question 201: Name the Brewers 22-year-old 1978 All-Star pitcher who finished the season with an 18-12 record.
- a) Jerry Augustine
- b) Mike Caldwell
- c) Lary Sorensen
- d) Bill Travers

Question 202: What Brewer pitching workhorse led the American League in games pitched in 1988 and 1989?
- a) Mark Clear
- b) Chuck Crim
- c) Mike Fetters
- d) Doug Henry

Question 203: What Brewers starter holds the franchise record for lowest season ERA of 2.36?
- a) Mike Caldwell
- b) Pete Vuckovich
- c) CC Sabathia
- d) Ben Sheets

Question 204: What Brewers starter holds the franchise record for best single season win/loss percentage?
- a) Mike Caldwell
- b) Cal Eldred
- c) CC Sabathia
- d) Jim Slaton

Question 205: Which pitching staff had the lowest team ERA

in the history of the Brewers franchise with 3.38?
- a) 1971
- b) 1981
- c) 1982
- d) 2007

Question 206: What General Manager with the nickname "Trader" replaced Marvin Milkes in 1970?

Question 207: What Brewers manager was fired after the Brewers 9-3 loss to the Boston Red Sox at Fenway Park on May 27, 1972?

Question 208: What popular ex-player took over managing the Brewers in 1972?

Question 209: Who took over as Brewers General Manager in October of 1972?

Question 210: Who joined Bud Selig and President George W. Bush for Miller Park's first pitch ceremony on April 6, 2001?

Question 211: In 1978, who became the first Brewer to be voted to the starting lineup of the All-Star Game?

Question 212: In 2004, who became the fifth Brewer to hit for the cycle?

Question 213: How many hits did the Brewers collect in their August 28, 1992, win over the Toronto Blue Jays? Hints: It was a franchise record and the final score was 22-2.
- a) 23
- b) 25
- c) 28
- d) 31

Question 214: On April 12, 1980, two Brewers hit grand slams in the second inning against the Boston Red Sox. Name the two sluggers who helped the Brewers secure the 18-1 win.
 a) Cecil Cooper and Ben Oglivie
 b) Cecil Cooper and Don Money
 c) Robin Yount and Larry Hisle
 d) Paul Molitor and Gorman Thomas

Question 215: What do Brewers Kevin Riemer and John Briggs have in common?
 a) Both hit pinch-hit grand slams
 b) Both hit four doubles in one game
 c) They are the only two Brewers to have six hits in one game
 d) They are the only two Brewers to commit three errors in one game

Question 216: Brewers' manager George Bamberger suffered a heart attack on March 6, 1980. Buck Rodgers filled in until Bamberger returned only three months later and helped the Brewers compile what June record?
 a) 14-14
 b) 15-13
 c) 16-12
 d) 18-10

Question 217: Name the three Brewers who had more than 100 RBI in 1980.

Question 218: Name the three key players that General Manager Harry Dalton picked up from the St. Louis Cardinals at the 1980 annual winter meetings.

Question 219: On August 16, 1980, Robin Yount became one of the youngest players to ever reach the 1,000th hit plateau. At what age did Yount accomplish this feat?

a) 23
b) 24
c) 25
d) 26

Question 220: What Brewer played in all 162 games in the 1980 season?
a) Cecil Cooper
b) Ben Oglivie
c) Gorman Thomas
d) Robin Yount

Question 221: What Brewers pitcher once had three balks in one game?
a) Mike Birkbeck
b) Bob Gibson
c) Eric Plunk
d) Pete Vuckovich

Question 222: On May 9, 1984, the Brewers lost a heartbreaking extra-innings game to the Chicago White Sox. The game played at Comiskey Park started on May 8 but was suspended during extra innings because of a league curfew and played out the following evening. The game lasted eight hours and six minutes. How many innings did the Brewers and White Sox battle each other?
a) 17
b) 21
c) 25
d) 27

Question 223: Who was the first Brewer to become an All-Star?

Question 224: What was the final score of the 2002 All-Star Game at Miller Park?

Question 225: Who hit a walk-off single in the bottom of the 11th inning on September 29, 2007, to beat the San Diego Padres and clinch the Brewers first winning season since 1992?
- a) Ryan Braun
- b) Craig Counsell
- c) Tony Gwynn, Jr.
- d) Vinny Rottino

5 OCTOBER BASEBALL ANSWER KEY

181. B – Wayne Franklin, 2003.

182. B – Tommy Harper.

183. B – 2003.

184. Jim Slaton.

185. Danny Darwin, 1985.

186. In June, Mason moved into a trailer on top of County Stadium's scoreboard and insisted that he would not come down until the Brewers drew 40,000 fans at one of their home games. He lived in the trailer until August 16 when 44,387 fans filled County Stadium to watch the Brewers beat the Cleveland Indians 4-3.

187. Bill Parsons.

188. Graeme Lloyd.

189. Steve Woodward, who tied an American League record for most strikeouts in a Major League debut (tying Elmer Myers of the 1915 Philadelphia Athletics).

190. Dan Plesac. He went on to become the Brewers all-time save leader with 133.

191. Cecil Cooper (1979, 1980, 1982, 1983, 1985) and Paul Molitor (1980, 1985, 1988, 1991, 1992).

192. George Scott.

193. Don Sutton.

194. Ken Sanders.

195. Jim Slaton.

196. Yount (252), Jenkins (212), Thomas (208), Cooper (201), and Oglivie (176).

197. Mike Hegan, who retired as a Brewer in 1977 and spent the next 12 years as a radio broadcaster for the Brewers.

198. Danny Walton. His fast start created a fan frenzy as the first Brew Crew Bleacher Bums held a sign that read, "Walton Fan Club". Although Walton stayed hot in May, he hurt his knee and his career was never the same. Over the next nine seasons, he played only 145 Major League games.

199. They hit five triples in one game.

200. Sixto Lezcano, who hit Opening Day grand slams in 1978 and 1980.

201. C – Lary Sorensen.

202. B – Chuck Crim.

203. A – Mike Caldwell, 1978.

204. B – Cal Eldred, .846 in 1992 (11-2 record).

205. A – 1971.

206. Famous Frank "Trader" Lane.

207. Dave Bristol.

208. Del Crandell. Pitcher Skip Lockwood pitched a one-hitter against the New York Yankees in Crandell's managerial debut.

209. Jim Wilson.

210. Davey Lopes.

211. Don Money.

212. Chad Moeller. For years, Harley-Davidson Motorcycle promised a motorcycle for any Brewer who hit for the cycle. However, the company discontinued their promotion in 2004. As Moeller discussed missing the free motorcycle for his cycle at a press conference, manager Ned Yost wheeled a Trek mountain bicycle in and said, "Since we lost the Harley sponsorship, here's something. I found a bike out there, Chad!" Yost presented the bike to Moeller who then responded, "That's awesome! Safer for me, too."

213. D – 31.

214. B – Cecil Cooper and Don Money.

215. C – Riemer and Briggs are the only Brewers to have six hits in one game.

216. D – 18-10.

217. Cecil Cooper (122), Ben Oglivie (118) and Gorman Thomas (105). The Brewers became the first team since the 1948-49 Boston Red Sox to have three players hit 100 RBI in a season for two consecutive years. In 1979, Thomas knocked in 123, Cooper 106, and Sixto Lezcano 101.

218. Catcher Ted Simmons, starting pitcher Pete Vuckovich, and the all-time save leader in baseball at the time, Rollie Fingers.

219. B – 24.

220. C – Gorman Thomas.

221. A – Mike Birkbeck.

222. C – 25. Milwaukee actually scored three times in the top of the 21st inning . . . only to give up three in the bottom of the frame to keep the game going.

223. Third baseman Tommy Harper, 1970.

224. It was 7-7. The infamous tie left many fans bewildered, chanting, "Let them play! Let them play!" New York Yankees manager Joe Torre and World Series Champions Arizona Diamondbacks manager Bob Brenly ran out of pitchers, so Commissioner Bud Selig declared the game a tie after 11 innings. "Nobody wanted to play more than I did, but I have to balance the concerns and hopes of the fans against the welfare of the players and the game. And every so often you get caught in a really difficult and sensitive situation. This is why they have a commissioner, because somebody has to make those decisions," said Selig. He later added, "This will never happen again."

225. D – Vinny Rottino, who was born and raised in Racine, WI and played college baseball for UW-LaCrosse. Studying to be a pharmacist, Rottino signed as a free agent in 2003. He was the Brewers minor league player of the year in 2004.

Got your October total? Here's how it breaks down:

Walk-off bomb to win Game 7 and MVP honors
= 40-45

Won a ring in a thrilling seven-game series
= 35-39

Good job – you did enough to get the ring
= 30-35

Lost a tough seven-game series
= 25-29

They're calling you the new Bill Buckner
= 00-24

Those of you who made it the entire season without making a trip to the minors, nice job! Feel free to take a quick glance at Chapter Six if you're curious ... otherwise, skip ahead to Chapter Seven and good luck in the Hall of Fame balloting!

"Anybody with ability can play in the big leagues. To last as long as I did with the skills I had, with the numbers I produced, was a triumph of the human spirit."
— *Bob Uecker*

6 MINOR LEAGUES

Can't find the strike zone? Gone hitless in your last 15 at bats? Bobbling too many groundballs? Well, your poor play has resulted in the Brewers sending you down to the Class-A Wisconsin Timber Rattlers in Grand Chute, Wisconsin. You will be playing your games at Fox Cities Stadium in front of sellout crowds of 5,500 fans! Score well here and you will get called back up to the Big Show.

Question 226: What number did Brewers Hall of Famer Robin Yount wear?

Question 227: True or False: The Brewers dugout at County Stadium was on the third base side.

Question 228: What year did the Brewers lose to the St. Louis Cardinals in the World Series?

Question 229: What Brewers closer is famous for his waxed handlebar moustache?

Question 230: Who was raised in Eden, Wisconsin, played college baseball at UW-Oshkosh, and played his entire Major League career with the Brewers from 1976 until 1992?

Question 231: What legendary Brewers announcer starred in 1980s sitcom Mr. Belvidere and the films Major League, Major League II, and Major League. Back to the Minors?

Question 232: What former Milwaukee Brewers owner is currently the commissioner of Major League Baseball?

Question 233: True or False: Cecil Cooper was a left-handed hitter.

Question 234: What number did Paul Molitor wear?

Question 235: What 5' 11", 270-lb Brewers slugger won the 2009 Home Run Derby in St. Louis?

6 MINOR LEAGUES ANSWER KEY

226. 19.

227. False.

228. 1982.

229. Rollie Fingers. It's been said Fingers first grew the moustache to get a $300 bonus from Oakland Athletics owner Charles O. Finley.

230. Jim Gantner. After being inducted into Miller Park's Walk of Fame, an MLB.com article reported Gantner stated, "The game is over with, but the memories will last forever, and that's what's so special about this night. I was very fortunate to play my entire career with the Milwaukee Brewers. Not many people get lucky enough to be about to play for their state team."

231. Bob Uecker.

232. Bud Selig.

233. True.

234. 4.

235. Prince Fielder.

Got your Minor Leagues total? Here's how it breaks down:

> You earned your way back to The Show
> = 8 or Higher

> The dreaded outright release
> = 7 or Fewer

Sorry my friends, but if you've been released then here's what you have to look forward to: six seasons of semi-pro ball, but your dreams of playing in the Bigs will go unfulfilled, swept away like the peanut shells and Big League Chew gum wrappers from last night's game.

"No one ever accomplishes something like this [Hall of Fame] without a lot of help from good people along the way ... I never dreamed of being in the Hall of Fame. Standing here with all these great players was beyond any of my dreams."

— *Robin Yount*

7 HALL OF FAME

Do you have what it takes to be a Brewers trivia Hall of Famer? A player needs to receive 75% of the Baseball Writer's Association of America votes in order to be inducted into the Hall of Fame. Therefore, if you answer 15 of the 20 HOF questions correctly, you may consider yourself enshrined in the Brew Crew IQ Hall of Fame!

Question 235: What Brewers pitcher lost the most games (20) in one season?
   a)   Chris Capuano
   b)   Jamie Cocanower
   c)   Jamie Navarro
   d)   Clyde Wright

Question 236: Who holds the Brewers record for most innings pitched in a season (314.1)?
   a)   Mike Caldwell
   b)   Jim Colborn
   c)   CC Sabathia

d) Lary Sorensen

Question 237: What pitcher surrendered 106 walks in 1975?
a) Jerry Augustine
b) Pete Broberg
c) Jim Slaton
d) Bill Travers

Question 238: Who hit the franchise's first pinch-hit home run in 1970?
a) Tito Francona
b) Ted Kubiak
c) Jerry McNertney
d) Roberto Pena

Question 239: Who shared the 1973 Brewers Player of the Year Award with George Scott?

Question 240: Who was the Brewers lone representative at the 1971 All-Star Game at Tiger Stadium?

Question 241: What Brewers catcher represented Milwaukee at the 1974 All-Star Game at Three Rivers Stadium in Pittsburgh?

Question 242: Who became the Brewers first 20-game winner when he tossed a three-hitter at County Stadium against the New York Yankees on September 26, 1973?

Question 243: What Kansas City Royals pitcher tossed a no-hitter against the Brewers at County Stadium on June 19, 1974?

Question 244: On July 20, 1976, Hank Aaron blasted his 755th and last career home run against what California Angels pitcher?

MILWAUKEE BREWERS IQ

Question 245: Who was the Brewers lone 1972 All-Star Game representative?

Question 246: What legendary pitcher out-dueled Brewers' ace Bill Travers 1-0 on April 12, 1977?

Question 247: What Brewers pitcher struck out 14 New York Yankees on April 12, 1978?

Question 248: Robin Yount played in a franchise record 2,856 games for the Brewers – exactly 1,000 more games than the man who played in the second most games in franchise history. Who is second on that list with 1,856 games played for the Brewers?

Question 249: The Milwaukee Brewers played their first game on April 7, 1970, at County Stadium. What pitcher lost the 12-0 decision to Andy Messersmith and the California Angels?

Question 250: What Brewers pitcher picked up the franchise's first win on April 11, 1970, against the Chicago White Sox at Comiskey Park?

Question 251: What Brewers pitcher flirted with history when he threw 7.1 innings of perfect baseball and 8.1 innings of no-hit baseball during his 2-0 win over the Cleveland Indians in 1988?

Question 252: Who hit the first Brewers home run at Miller Park?

Question 253: How many days was the 1973 season opener delayed and why?

Question 254: Who hit the franchise's first grand slam home run, which just happened to be an inside-the-parker?
  a) Tito Francona
  b) Ted Kubiak
  c) Jerry McNertney
  d) Roberto Pena

7 HALL OF FAME ANSWER KEY

235. D – Clyde Wright, 1974.

236. B – Jim Colborn, 1973.

237. B – Pete Broberg.

238. C – Jerry McNertney.

239. Davey May.

240. Marty Pattin, who unfortunately did not play in the game.

241. Darrell Porter, who was later traded to the Royals and eventually landed in St. Louis where his clutch hits earned him the 1982 World Series MVP Award – against his former team, when the Cardinals beat the Brewers in seven games.

242. Jim Colborn.

243. Steve Busby.

244. Dick Drago – Hammerin' Hank's home run helped lift the Brewers to a 6-2 win.

245. Catcher Ellie Rodriguez.

246. Jim Palmer pitched a complete game two-hitter for the Baltimore Orioles. This was the Brewers home opener and temperatures reached as high as 83 degrees.

247. Moose Haas. He fanned Reggie Jackson four times!

248. Paul Molitor.

249. Lew Krausse.

250. John O'Donoghue.

251. Odell Jones.

252. Jeromy Burnitz.

253. Four days because of a 13-inch snowstorm.

254. D – Roberto Pena.

Got your Hall of Fame total? Here's how it breaks down:

Congrats! You're a Hall of Famer
= 15-20

You came close, still on the ballot next year
= 10-14

No dice, you're off next year's ballot
= 00-09

Remember it's not whether you won or lost, it's how you played the game!

"Baseball hasn't forgotten me. I go to a lot of Old Timers games and I haven't lost a thing. I sit in the bullpen and let people throw things at me. Just like old times."
— *Bob Uecker*

8 ULTIMATE STUMPERS

So you think you had a great year, huh? Your agent Scott Boras has negotiated a new contract for you. Let's see if you earn a signing bonus by answering these ultimate stumpers – earn a (figurative) $2 million bonus for each question you get right, up to $10 million total. Not bad!

Question 255: It has been estimated that it would take this many baseballs to fill Miller Park.

Question 256: The weight of Miller Park is equivalent to how many 16-pound bowling balls?

Question 257: In 1998, rookie Bronswell Patrick became the first Brewer pitcher to hit a home run since 1971. What pitcher knocked one out of the park in 1971?

Question 258: Who is the author's all-time favorite Brewers name to say?

Question 259: Can you name the 12 Brewers who fans voted to the 20th Anniversary Team? Hint: three pitchers, eight position players, and one designated hitter.

8 ULTIMATE STUMPERS ANSWER KEY

255. 4,655,926,995!

256. 62,500,000!

257. Skip Lockwood.

258. Billy Joe Robideaux (pronounced with long O's Ro-bid-do).

259. Pitchers: Mike Caldwell, Rollie Fingers, Pete Vuckovich; Catcher: Charlie Moore; First Base: Cecil Cooper; Second Base: Jim Gantner; Third Base: Paul Molitor; Shortstop: Robin Yount; Outfield: Sixto Lezcano, Gorman Thomas, Ben Oglivie; and Designated Hitter: Hank Aaron.

JOEL KATTE

Got your bonus total? Here's how it breaks down.

Cha-Ching! $10 Million Bonus
= 5 for 5

Nice! A cool $8 Million Bonus
= 4 for 5

Still serious cash! $6 Million Bonus
= 3 for 5

Not bad! Looking at $4 Million Bonus
= 2 for 5

Hey, it's still a $2 Million Bonus
= 1 for 5

Sorry, no bonus this time
= 0 for 5

ABOUT THE AUTHOR

Joel Katte is an elementary school principal for Fayette County Public Schools in Lexington, Kentucky.

Joel loves taking road trips with his family. He and his family enjoy hiking, biking, swimming, and playing tennis. During summers, Joel also plays baseball for the Lexington Bombers in the Bluegrass Baseball League.

For updates follow Joel on Twitter @JoelKatte or visit:

www.KentuckyDerbyIQ.blogspot.com

www.CountyStadiumKid.blogspot.com

JoelKatte@gmail.com

ACKNOWLEDGEMENTS

I wholeheartedly thank:

The Klessig Family for providing their vacation rental by owner lake house "Saxon Sunrise," the best writing space I have ever encountered.

My friends Dan Flagstad, Heinz Mueller, and Ron Glodoski for their steadfast support.

My mom and dad for their love, sacrifice, and encouragement to have "Big League" dreams and also for their willingness to take me to County Stadium early for batting practice and stay late for autographs.

My children Wesley, Holly, and Daisy for inspiring me to strive to be the man and father they deserve me to be and also for their eagerness to love the Milwaukee Brewers and Bernie Brewer as much as I do.

My awesome, dynamic wife, Dawn, for her love, respect, and trust; she is and always will be the best thing that has ever happened to me.

REFERENCES

Baseball-almanac.com

BaseballHallofFame.org

Baseball-reference.com

ESPN.com

MLB.com

Milwaukee.Brewers.MLB.com

TheBaseballPage.com

JOEL KATTE

Visit us on the web to learn more about Black Mesa and our authors:

www.blackmesabooks.com

Or contact us via email:

admin@blackmesabooks.com

JOEL KATTE

Green Bay Packers IQ:
The Ultimate Test of True Fandom

JOEL KATTE

Now available from Black Mesa Publishing.

"Football is a great deal like life in that it teaches that work, sacrifice, perseverance, competitive drive, selflessness and respect for authority is the price that each and every one of us must pay to achieve any goal that is worthwhile."

— *Vince Lombardi*

1 THROUGH THE YEARS

Starting with the "Iron Man" era all the way through the 2012 season, the first 190 questions are likely to be as tough as the gritty men who played this great game without any helmets. If you make it through with only a few injuries and fumbles, you will be in good shape for a glorious Super Bowl finish!

THE "IRON MAN" ERA

Question 1: The Green Bay Packers were founded in the editorial room of the *Green Bay Press-Gazette*. The meeting was called by Curly Lambeau and George Calhoun. In what year was this great American franchise formed?
   a) 1909
   b) 1919
   c) 1920
   d) 1921

Question 2: When the Packers played their first game, the league was not called the NFL. What was the name of the league?

Question 3: When the Green Bay Packers and Chicago Bears rivalry started, what were the Bears known as?
   a) Wildcats
   b) Bearcats
   c) Staleys
   d) Ditkas

Question 4: Andrew B. Turnbull was the Packers first what?
   a) Quarterback
   b) Punter
   c) President
   d) Coach

Question 5: How many regular season games did it take before the Packers beat the Chicago Bears?
   a) Two
   b) Three
   c) Four
   d) Five

Question 6: The Packers first played in City Stadium. What was its initial capacity?
   a) 6,000
   b) 12,000
   c) 20,000
   d) 26,000

Question 7: J.E. Clair of Acme Packing Company first owned the Packers franchise, but he turned it over to the league in

1922 after the team was disciplined for not obeying league rules. The franchise was purchased back for $250. How much of that did general manager and coach Curly Lambeau pay?
  a) 50
  b) 100
  c) 150
  d) 250

Question 8: In 1922, the Packers endured bad weather and poor attendance, so a public non-profit corporation was set up to save the team. How much money was raised?
  a) $1,000
  b) $2,500
  c) $10,000
  d) $25,000

Question 9: In 1927, the Packers stunned critics when they beat what "Big Town" franchise 13-0?

Question 10: In 1929, the Packers win their first NFL title. What was their final record?

ANSWER KEY

Question 1: B. 1919

Question 2: American Professional Football Association

Question 3: C. Staleys

Question 4: C. President

Question 5: C. 4

Question 6: A. 6,000

Question 7: A. $50

Question 8: B. $2,500

Question 9: New York Yankees (No, it was not the same New York Yankees featuring Babe Ruth and the Bronx Bombers.)

Question 10: 12-0-1

Keep a running tally of your correct answers!

Number correct: ___ / 10

Overall correct: ___ / 10

THE THIRTIES

Question 11: The Packers won their second NFL title with a 10-3-1 record. What year was this?
a) 1930
b) 1932
c) 1933
d) 1934

Question 12: True or False: The Packers won three consecutive NFL titles.

Question 13: In 1932, the Packers impressive winning streak was snapped after how many consecutive wins?
a) 12
b) 14
c) 18
d) 22

Question 14: In 1932, the Packers posted an impressive 10-3-1 record; however, the Chicago Bears won the NFL title that year. What was the Bears record?
a) 11-2-1
b) 10-2-2
c) 8-4-2
d) 7-1-6

Question 15: What Packers legend from Alabama became one of the best receivers of all-time?

Question 16: What incident in 1934 almost caused the Packers to fold?

Question 17: In 1936, the first NFL draft was held. Whom did the Packers select as their first ever number one draft choice?
 a) B. Johnny Blood McNally
 b) T. Cal Hubbard
 c) Russ Letlow
 d) Tony Mandrich
 e) Mike Michalske

Question 18: In 1936, the Packers won their fourth NFL title. This was the first title under the playoff system. What team did the Packers defeat 21-6 to win this title?

Question 19: Where was the 1936 title game played?

Question 20: In 1938, the Packers reached the title game but lost 23-17. What franchise that still exists today won the 1938 NFL title?

Question 21: The Packers won the 1939 NFL title game 27-0. Where was this game played?
 a) Green Bay
 b) New York
 c) Chicago
 d) Milwaukee

MILWAUKEE BREWERS IQ

ANSWER KEY

Question 11: A. 1930

Question 12: True

Question 13: D. 22 consecutive wins

Question 14: D. 7-1-6 (Yes, six tie games!)

Question 15: Don Hutson

Question 16: A fan fell from the stands at the old City Stadium. The fan sued and was awarded $5,000. After the insurance company went out of business, the Packers went into receivership and eventually were saved when local Green Bay business owners raised $15,000.

Question 17: Russ Letlow from the University of San Francisco

Question 18: Boston Redskins

Question 19: New York's Polo Grounds

Question 20: New York Giants

Question 21: D. Milwaukee

Keep a running tally of your correct answers!

Number correct: ___ / 11

Overall correct: ___ / 21

THE FORTIES

Question 22: The Packers and the Bears tied for the 1941 Western Division title. Who won the playoff game 33-14?

Question 23: 1n 1944, the Packers defeated the New York Giants 14-7 at the Polo Grounds to win their sixth NFL title. Name the Packer who scored both touchdowns.

Question 24: In 1945, Don Hutson set the all-time single quarter scoring record with 29 points, helping the Packers beat Detroit 57-21 in Milwaukee. How did he score the 29 points?

Question 25: In 1949, the Packers again faced financial woes, but they played a Thanksgiving intra-squad game at old City Stadium and raised funds. How much money did they raise?
   a) $25,000
   b) $35,000
   c) $50,000
   d) $60,000

MILWAUKEE BREWERS IQ

ANSWER KEY

Question 22: Bears

Question 23: Ted Fritsch

Question 24: Don Hutson scored 29 points in one quarter by catching four touchdown passes and kicking five extra points.

Question 25: C. $25,000

    Keep a running tally of your correct answers!

        Number correct: ___ / 4

        Overall correct: ___ / 25

THE FIFTIES

Question 26: In 1950, Curly Lambeau resigned to become vice president and coach of what team?
 a) New York Giants
 b) Boston Redskins
 c) Chicago Cardinals
 d) Houston Oilers

Question 27: In 1950, the Packers appeared to be in good financial standing when their stock drive netted how much money?
 a) $105,000
 b) $112,000
 c) $118,000
 d) $124,000

Question 28: In 1953, the Packers played in what new stadium on September 27?

Question 29: In 1953, Gene Ronzani resigned as coach. Name the two co-coaches who took over.

Question 30: The "New" Packers introduced new uniforms featuring what new color?

Question 31: Name the former Marquette University coach who became the Packers coach in 1954.

Question 32: In what year was construction completed on City Stadium just in time for an Opening Day 21-17 victory over the Chicago Bears?

a) 1955
b) 1956
c) 1957
d) 1958

Question 33: The Packers' 1956 4-8 record was actually better than their 1957 record. What was their 1957 record?
a) 4-7-1
b) 3-9
c) 2-10
d) 1-11

Question 34: Assistant coach Ray "Scooter" McLean took over as head coach in 1958 but resigned after the Packers worst year in franchise history. What was the Packers record under McLean?

Question 35: Iconic coach Vince Lombardi was named the Packers head coach and general manager in February 1959. Lombardi was the offensive assistant coach for what team before coming to Green Bay?
a) New York Giants
b) New York Jets
c) Buffalo Bills
d) University of Notre Dame

Question 36: In his first season with the Packers, coach Vince Lombardi helped the Packers post a winning record of 7-5. This was the Packers first winning record in how many years?
a) 7
b) 9
c) 11
d) 12

JOEL KATTE

ANSWER KEY

Question 26: C. Chicago Cardinals

Question 27: C. $118,000

Question 28: Milwaukee County Stadium

Question 29: Hugh Devore and Ray "Scooter" Mclean

Question 30: Green

Question 31: Lisle Blackbourn

Question 32: C. 1957

Question 33: B. 3-9

Question 34: 1-10-1

Question 35: A. New York Giants

Question 36: D. 12 years

    Keep a running tally of your correct answers!

        Number correct: ___ / 11

        Overall correct: ___ / 36

THE SIXTIES

Question 37: In 1960, the Packers won the Western Division title for the first time since what year?
- a) 1940
- b) 1942
- c) 1944
- d) 1946

Question 38: The Packers lost the 1960 NFL title game 17-13 to what team?
- a) Giants
- b) Jets
- c) Eagles
- d) Redskins

Question 39: Name the Packers legend who scored an NFL record 176 points in 1960.

Question 40: The record of 176 points scored in a single season stood until what year?
- a) 1986
- b) 1991
- c) 2003
- d) 2006

Question 41: In 1961, the Packers routed the New York Giants for their seventh NFL championship. What was the final score?

Question 42: What was significant about where the Packers 1961 title game was played?

Question 43: In 1962, the Packers again beat the Giants 16-7 in the NFL title game to win their second straight championship. Where was this game played?

Question 44: In 1965, Packers' founder and first coach E.L. "Curly" Lambeau passed away on June 1. City Stadium was renamed Lambeau Field on September 11. How old was Lambeau when he passed away?
 a) 61
 b) 64
 c) 67
 d) 71

Question 45: What was significant about the Packers 13-10 win over the Baltimore Colts in the 1965 Western Conference playoff game?

Question 46: Who kicked the game winning 25-yard field goal in the 1965 13-10 Western Conference win over the Colts?

Question 47: In 1967, the Packers won the first "Super Bowl" when they defeated the AFL's Chiefs in Los Angeles. What was the final score?
 a) 24-17
 b) 35-10
 c) 17-10
 d) 28-17

Question 48: In 1967, the Packers beat the Dallas Cowboys 21-17 to win their third consecutive NFL title. What was the nickname given to this game? HINT: The temperature was 13 degrees below zero.

Question 49: Who scored the last-minute 1-yard touchdown to beat the Cowboys in this historic game?

Question 50: In 1968, the Packers won the second ever "Super Bowl" with a 33-14 win in Miami. Who did they beat to secure another NFL title?
 a) Oakland Raiders
 b) Kansas City Chiefs
 c) New York Giants
 d) Miami Dolphins

Question 51: Vince Lombardi resigned as Packers coach after the 1968 season. He remained in Green Bay as the Packers general manager. However, in 1969 he resigned his role as general manager to become part-owner, executive vice-president, and head coach of what NFL team?
 a) Oakland Raiders
 b) Kansas City Chiefs
 c) Washington Redskins
 d) New York Jets

Question 52: Name the Packers head coach who replaced Vince Lombardi.

ANSWER KEY

Question 37: C. 1944

Question 38: C. Eagles

Question 39: Paul Hornung

Question 40: D. 2006 LaDanian Tomlinson broke the record with his 30th touchdown of the season.

Question 41: 37-0

Question 42: This was the first title game played in Green Bay.

Question 43: New York's Yankee Stadium

Question 44: C. 67

Question 45: The 13-10 win was the first Packers game in overtime in franchise history.

Question 46: Don Chandler

Question 47: B. 35-10

Question 48: "Ice Bowl"

Question 49: Bart Starr scored a last-minute 1-yard touchdown on a quarterback sneak.

Question 50: A. Oakland Raiders

Question 51: C. Washington Redskins

Question 52: Phil Bengston

MILWAUKEE BREWERS IQ

Keep a running tally of your correct answers!

Number correct: ___ / 16

Overall correct: ___ / 52

THE SEVENTIES

Question 53: Packers legend Vince Lombardi passed away on September 3, 1970. How old was he?
   a) 54
   b) 57
   c) 59
   d) 61

Question 54: After coach Bengston resigned in 1970, this coach from the University of Missouri became the Packers head coach and general manager in 1971.

Question 55: In 1972, the Packers finished 10-4 and won the division title. When was the last time they had won their division?
   a) 1967
   b) 1968
   c) 1969
   d) 1970

Question 56: Despite winning their divisional title in 1972, the Packers title hopes ended when they lost 16-3 in the playoffs. What team did the Packers lose to?
   a) Kansas City Chiefs
   b) Denver Broncos
   c) Washington Redskins
   d) Miami Dolphins

Question 57: Dan Devine resigned as head coach in 1974. What was his combined record for the 1973 and 1974 seasons?
   a) 11-17

b) 14-14
c) 11-15-2
d) 12-15-1

Question 58: Bart Starr was named the Packers head coach and general manager in 1974 but unfortunately he was never able to replicate the same success he'd had on the field as a player while serving in this new capacity. Starr never won an NFL title coaching, but he had no problem winning as QB. How many NFL titles did he win as quarterback for the Packers?

a) 3
b) 4
c) 5
d) 6

ANSWER KEY

Question 53: B. 57

Question 54: Dan Devine

Question 55: A. 1967

Question 56: C. Redskins

Question 57: C. 11-15-2

Question 58: C. Five titles

Keep a running tally of your correct answers!

Number correct: ___ / 6

Overall correct: ___ / 58

THE EIGHTIES

Question 59: Judge Robert J. Parins was elected Packers President in 1982. He replaced Dominic Olejniczak. What was significant about Parins taking over?

Question 60: In what year did Bart Starr stop being the Packers head coach?
 a) 1981
 b) 1982
 c) 1983
 d) 1984

Question 61: What Packers legend signed a five-year head coaching contract in 1984?

Question 62: In 1985, the Packers added 72 private boxes at Lambeau Field bringing its capacity up to what?
 a) 52,357
 b) 56,926
 c) 58,782
 d) 60,711

Question 63: What year did the Packers generate their first $2,000,000 annual profit?
 a) 1986
 b) 1987
 c) 1988
 d) 1989

Question 64: In 1986, the Packers created the Green Bay Packers Foundation to do what?

Question 65: In 1988, coach Forrest Gregg resigned to become the coach at his alma mater. What school did he attend and later become head coach at?
   a) Notre Dame
   b) University of Mississippi
   c) Southern Methodist University
   d) University of Florida

Question 66: Name the Cleveland Browns offensive coordinator who signed a five-year contract to be Green Bay's next head coach?

Question 67: After Judge Parins retired as president, who was elected to be the next president and CEO of Packer Corporation?

Question 68: In 1989, the Packers released plans to create 1,920 club seats. Where did they place these seats?
   a) North end zone
   b) South end zone
   c) East 50 yard line
   d) West 50 yard line

Question 69: In addition to the addition of the club seats, the Packers added 36 additional boxes. What was the estimate of the total cost of the projects?
   a) $6,500,000
   b) $7,300,000
   c) $7,800,000
   d) $8,200,000

MILWAUKEE BREWERS IQ

ANSWER KEY

Question 59: Parins became the Packers' first full-time CEO in franchise history.

Question 60: 1983

Question 61: Forrest Gregg

Question 62: B. 56,926

Question 63: C. 1986 (One year later the Packers reported over $3,000,000 in profits.)

Question 64: To make a commitment to contributing to charities.

Question 65: C. Southern Methodist University

Question 66: Lindy Infante

Question 67: Bob Harlan

Question 68: B. South end zone

Question 69: D. $8,200,000

Keep a running tally of your correct answers!

Number correct: ___ / 11

Overall correct: ___ / 69